How to Draw the Life and Times of
Martin Van Buren

Roderic Schmidt

The Rosen Publishing Group's
PowerKids Press™
New York

To my mother

Published in 2006 by The Rosen Publishing Group, Inc.
29 East 21st Street, New York, NY 10010

First Edition

Editors: Melissa Acevedo and Orli Zuravicky
Layout Design: Julio A. Gil

Illustrations: All illustrations by Elana Davidian.
Photo Credits: pp. 4, 20, 24 Library of Congress Prints and Photographs Division; pp. 7, 8, 12 © Bettmann/Corbis; pp. 9, 26 © Lee Snider; Lee Snider/Corbis; p. 10 Beer's Schoharie County Atlas, 1866. Provided by Office of General Services of New York; p. 14 U.S. Senate Collection; p. 16 © One Mile Up, Inc.; p.18 courtesy of the American Numismatic Society; p. 22 National Numismatic Collection, Smithsonian Institution; p. 28 National Portrait Gallery, Smithsonian Institution.

Library of Congress Cataloging-in-Publication Data

Schmidt, Roderic.
How to draw the life and times of Martin Van Buren / Roderic Schmidt.
    p. cm. — (A kid's guide to drawing the presidents of the United States of America)
Includes bibliographical references and index.
ISBN 1-4042-2985-X (lib. bdg.)
1. Van Buren, Martin, 1782–1862—Juvenile literature. 2. Presidents—United States—Biography—Juvenile literature. 3. Drawing—Technique—Juvenile literature. I. Title. II. Series.

E387.S36 2006
973.5'7'092—dc22

2004017220

Manufactured in the United States of America

Contents

Meet Martin Van Buren

Martin Van Buren was born on December 5, 1782, in Kinderhook, New York. His parents, Abraham and Maria, ran a small farm and bar on their property. Van Buren's family could only afford basic education, so he attended the local school. At age 14 he began

working as a clerk in a law office. Van Buren worked hard to learn how to be a lawyer.

In 1803, at the age of 20, he passed his exams and became a lawyer. As a lawyer Van Buren became involved in New York politics. The two major political parties in America at that time were the Democratic-Republicans and the Federalists. Van Buren supported the Democratic-Republican Party, which wanted the state governments to be stronger than the federal government. The Federalist Party, which mostly ran New York's government at the time, wanted the federal government to be stronger than the state governments. From 1808 to 1820, Van Buren helped organize New York's Democratic-Republicans to win the government back from the Federalists. He served in the New York state senate from 1812 to 1820 and in the U.S. Senate from 1821 to 1828. He also spent much time helping Andrew Jackson, a friend and fellow Democratic-Republican, campaign for the presidency. In 1828, he returned to New York and was elected governor. However, soon after Van Buren took office as governor, Jackson was elected president. Van Buren resigned as New York's governor to serve as President Jackson's secretary of state and then his vice president. Van Buren ran for president in 1836 and won.

You will need the following supplies to draw the life and times of Martin Van Buren:

✓ A sketch pad   ✓ An eraser   ✓ A pencil   ✓ A ruler

These are some of the shapes and drawing terms you need to know:

Horizontal Line	——	Squiggly Line	
Oval		Trapezoid	
Rectangle		Triangle	
Shading		Vertical Line	
Slanted Line	/	Wavy Line	

Presidency and Later Life

Martin Van Buren was inaugurated as the eighth president in 1837. He faced many problems. The fall of the country's economy, called the Panic of 1837, began right after he took office. Van Buren had trouble with Mexico and Great Britain, who were fighting over land the United States felt belonged to them. The issue of slavery was also becoming a problem among the states. Many people blamed Van Buren for these problems, and he was not reelected for another term.

Van Buren stayed active in politics even after his presidency ended. He ran for president a third time, in 1848, but was once again unsuccessful. Through the years, he realized that slavery was a big problem for the country. He used his experience and influence as a former president to try to solve this problem.

From 1848 until his death in 1862, Van Buren led an active retirement. In 1854, he traveled to Europe. In his free time, he wrote down his life story. He spent most of his later years on his farm, Lindenwald, entertaining friends and being with his family.

This is a wood print of Martin Van Buren's presidential inauguration on March 4, 1837. In his inaugural address, he praised the writers of the Constitution and vowed to govern the country according to the "letter and spirit of the Constitution" as it was created by its framers.

Van Buren's New York

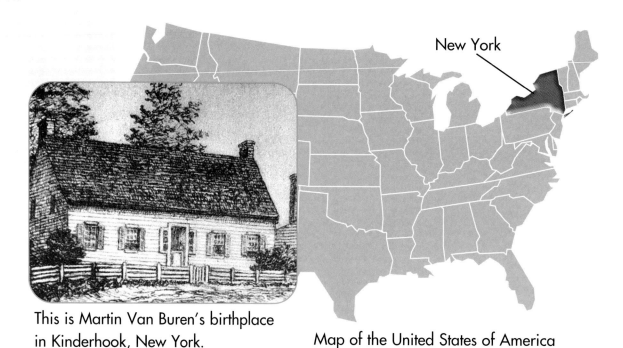

This is Martin Van Buren's birthplace in Kinderhook, New York.

Map of the United States of America

In the early 1800s, New York was becoming one of the wealthiest and most-populated states in the country. By 1830, about one out of every seven Americans was a New Yorker. New York state politicians began to realize how influential they could be in the federal government. New York was allowed more representation in the House of Representatives because of the state's large population. This meant that it had more votes.

Even before this growth in population, New York had been home to the Van Buren family. Their family tree can be traced back to the late 1600s, to the time when the Dutch still owned New York. Many Dutch families, like the Van Burens, settled in upstate New York along the Hudson River. In 1839, during his presidency, Van Buren bought farmland in Kinderhook, New York, the town in which he was born. There he built an estate that he named Lindenwald. He retired to Lindenwald after his term ended. This home is now a national historic area. Visitors can take tours of his house and learn more about him.

This photograph shows the library at Lindenwald, which was Martin Van Buren's favorite room. The library was also known as the gentlemen's room. Van Buren and his friends would gather there to play cards and talk.

Lawyer and Politician

Martin Van Buren started practicing law in 1803. As a lawyer he worked many long hours on cases in Albany's capitol building, shown here. While practicing law Van  Buren became heavily involved in politics. In time, he became a valuable and active member of the Democratic-Republican Party. His ties to the Democratic-Republican Party earned him a job as a government clerk for Columbia, New York, in 1808.

In 1812, Van Buren won the election for New York state senate. When he began his term, America was fighting Britain in the War of 1812. Van Buren approved of the war. As a state senator, he worked hard to get New York to support the war and the federal government. He served in the state senate until 1820. From 1816 to 1819, Van Buren also served as attorney general of New York, which meant that he represented the state in court and was the state's head lawyer.

1

To draw the New York State capitol building, start with a large rectangle. Add a rectangle and a trapezoid inside the large rectangle. These will be the front and side of the building.

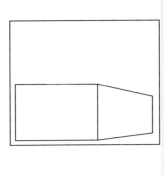

2

Add two triangles and draw a zigzag line to connect them. Then draw two vertical lines, a circle, and a curved shape above the circle as shown. Add the lines to the base of the rectangle.

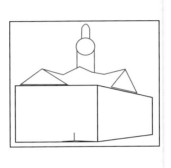

3

Erase extra lines. Draw a rectangle and connect it to the triangle with lines. Add the shape next to the triangle. Draw two ovals on the roof. Add a line on the right and a line at the bottom.

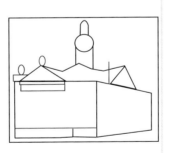

4

Draw four rectangles to make columns. Add lines to the right side of the building. Add the shapes to the roof.

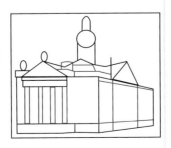

5

Erase the large rectangular guide and any lines inside the roof. Add more lines to the roof, including two rectangles for the chimneys. Draw rectangles and lines for the windows.

6

Add the chimneys inside the guides. Add railings as shown. Finish the columns. Add lines to the tower as shown. Add more lines to the building. Draw the door and stairs as shown.

7

Erase extra lines and the guides for the columns and chimneys. Add more lines to the stairs and railings. Add lines for details to the roof as shown. Add the door and window to the capitol.

8

Erase the guides around the statue and the small ornaments on the roof. Add more detail to the roof and windows as shown. Finish by shading. Nice work!

Organizing a Political Party

By 1813, Martin Van Buren came to believe that DeWitt Clinton, a powerful Democratic-Republican, put his own personal needs ahead of the good of the

people. To oppose Clinton, Van Buren organized a new group of Democratic-Republicans. New York City's Tammany Society, a group of rich and powerful men, joined Van Buren's political party. The Tammany members brought him connections to influential people. These people, called the Albany Regency, helped Van Buren's party gain power in New York's government.

Between 1817 and 1825, New York State built the Erie Canal, shown above. The canal made traveling across the state easier and cheaper. The canal was so popular that both Van Buren and Clinton supported it. Clinton was appointed canal commissioner, which meant that he was in charge of the project. However, the Albany Regency had DeWitt Clinton replaced by Martin Van Buren as canal commissioner in 1824.

1

Start by drawing a long rectangle. This will be your guide for drawing the Erie Canal.

2

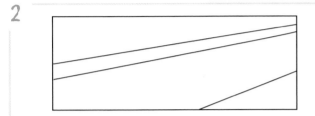

Add three slanted lines as shown. These will be the guides for the fence and the river.

3

Add two curved shapes inside the slanted lines you just made. These will be the base for the two boats in the river. Add a curved line to the front of the boat on the left.

4

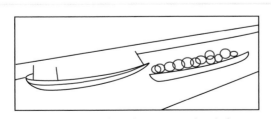

Add three lines to the shape on the left. Erase the slanted line between the first and last lines you just added. Draw a curved line inside the boat on the left. Draw many overlapping circles above the boat on the right.

5

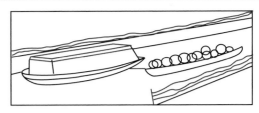

Add two long, squiggly lines. Make a roof for the boat on the left and add a small line to the back. Make a fence in the lower right corner using a slanted line and three squiggly lines. Connect the boats with a line.

6

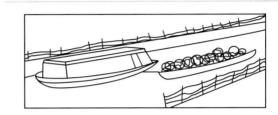

Draw rock shapes inside the circular guides you made in step 4. Add two slanted lines for the doorway of the larger boat. Add many slanted vertical lines to the fences.

7

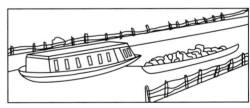

Draw shapes around the slanted lines you just made for the fence posts. Add a squiggly line for a bush. Next draw rectangles to make windows on the larger boat. Erase the circular guides in the smaller boat.

8

Finish the drawing by shading as shown. Your drawing looks great!

U.S. Senator

In 1821, Martin Van Buren was elected to the U.S. Senate. He moved to Washington, D.C., the capital of the United States. He spent much of his time trying to strengthen the Democratic-Republicans across the country. Van Buren saw political parties as the answer to the problems that slavery was causing. The northern and southern parts of the country constantly argued over the issue of slavery. People feared the United States might split into two separate countries. Van Buren thought that having Democratic-Republican party members scattered throughout the country could keep America together by smoothing out any differences between the arguing states.

In 1827, Van Buren began helping Andrew Jackson campaign for the presidency. Van Buren managed the campaign by using newspapers and meetings to keep people informed and excited. Without his help the Albany Regency would not have been able to convince New York Democrats to support Jackson.

1 The bust of Martin Van Buren is a statue of the upper part of his body and head. It was created by Ulric Stonewall Jackson Dunbar in 1894. Start the bust by drawing a rectangle as a guide.

2 Next draw three oval guides inside the rectangle as shown. These will be the guides for the head, the face, and the body of the bust of Martin Van Buren.

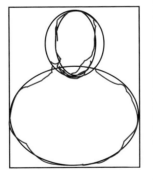

3 Draw squiggly lines inside the oval guides you just made for the body and head.

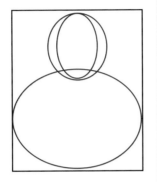

4 Erase the oval guides for the body and for the face. Add two wavy lines for the arms. Draw two curved shapes for hair on either side of the head. Add guides for the face as shown.

5 Erase the remaining head guide. Add slanted lines to make the jacket collar. Draw a line from the point of the collar to the bottom of the jacket. Draw the nose, eyes, and mouth using the guides.

6 Add more lines to the face and erase the guides. Add four circles for the buttons on the jacket. Add wavy lines inside the guides for the jacket you made in step 5.

7 Erase all extra lines. Add wavy lines to the hair. Add the remaining lines for the shirt. Draw wavy lines to show the folds in the jacket.

8 Erase the rectangle guide. Add more lines and shading to the eyes of the bust of Van Buren. Finish the drawing by shading in the jacket, hair, and collar. Good job!

From Governor to Cabinet Member

In 1828, Martin Van Buren ran for governor of New York. He also continued to campaign for Andrew Jackson. His efforts paid off in November 1828, when Jackson was elected president and Van Buren was elected governor. Governor Van Buren favored the Safety Fund Plan, which had rules for how money was given out in New York State. Twelve weeks after he took office as New York State's governor, Van Buren resigned to accept the position as Jackson's secretary of state.

As secretary of state, Van Buren handled trade agreements between America and other countries. He also tried to get the other cabinet members to stop acting out against President Jackson and to support him. After failing to get that support, Van Buren resigned as secretary of state. He explained that he felt the behavior of certain cabinet members was wrong. Ashamed, the rest of the cabinet resigned as well. Jackson was then able to appoint a new cabinet.

1

The Great Seal of New York State was created in 1882. When Van Buren was governor of New York, he was in charge of the seal. Begin drawing the seal by making three circles as shown.

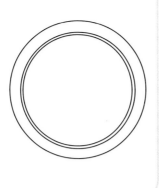

2

Add two horizontal lines across the inside circle for the guide of the ribbon. Draw the two six-sided shapes that will be the guides for the shield. Add the guides for the top of the shield and globe.

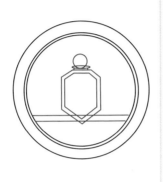

3

Add details to the shield as shown. Draw a triangle above the circle. This will be the guide for the eagle. Add two guides for the women.

4

Erase the shield guides. Draw ovals on the guides for the women. These will be guides for the women's clothing. Add the shape between their hands as shown.

5

Erase any extra lines. Add curved lines to the ribbon as shown. Draw the hair and the arms for the two women. Create the outline of an eagle inside the triangle.

6

Erase the guides for the ribbon, the eagle, and the women's arms. Add lines to the eagle. Draw clothing on the women. Add two rectangles for the sword and a curved shape for the flame.

7

Erase the remaining guides. Add lines to the clothing and globe. Add the scale for the woman on the right. Add the writing on the ribbon and inside the top of the seal. Add the scene to the shield.

8

Add squiggly lines around the edge of the circle. Finish by shading. Good job!

Vice President Van Buren

In 1832, Andrew Jackson was reelected president with Martin Van Buren as his vice president. Soon after  South Carolina claimed that states could nullify, or ignore, federal laws if they did not approve of them. Van Buren helped make South Carolina understand that states needed to follow the federal laws. South Carolina gave up on nullification.

The storage of the government's money became a problem for Jackson. President Jackson decided to close the government's central bank, the Second Bank of the United States. He felt that the bank's managers were not managing the government's money well. Van Buren thought this was a horrible decision. Even though he was against the decision to divide the money among private banks, Van Buren remained loyal to Jackson. The above banknote was issued in 1840 after Jackson's decision to take away the bank's charter.

1

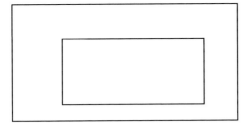

To draw the building of the Second Bank of the United States that appears on the top of the banknote, begin with a large rectangle. Draw a smaller rectangle inside the first.

2

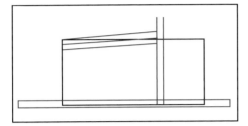

Add a long, thin rectangle underneath the smaller rectangle. Add two vertical lines coming out of the rectangle you just drew. Then add three slanted lines as shown.

3

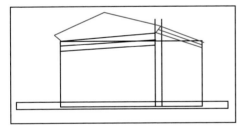

Using slanted lines, draw the shape on top of the slanted lines from step 2. Add three slanted lines on the right side of the building. The lines touch the new shape.

4

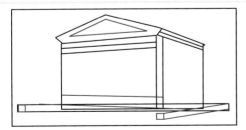

Erase extra lines. Draw a triangle in the shape you drew in step 3. Add lines to the bottom of the rectangles from steps 1 and 2 as shown. Add two small squares as shown.

5

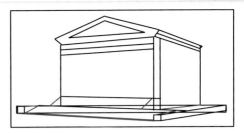

Add slanted lines as shown to connect the squares together. Add slanted lines for the stairs as shown. Add lines to the bottom of the side of the building as shown.

6

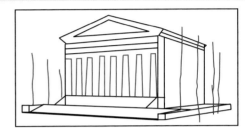

Erase extra lines. Using slanted lines, create eight columns. Then add three squiggly lines on the left side of the building and four on the right side. These will be for trees.

7

Add branches to the trees using curved lines. Using small rectangles and lines, add details to the top of the columns as shown.

8

Erase the large rectangular guide from step 1. Finish the drawing by shading. Notice how some parts of the building are darker than others. What a great job!

President Van Buren

At the close of Andrew Jackson's second term in 1836, Martin Van Buren ran for president and won. There were 26 states when he took office, as shown 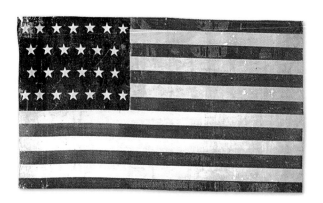 by the flag here. Van Buren tried to keep the country unified. Unfortunately, the Panic of 1837 struck early in Van Buren's term, and America's economy suffered. People feared their money was not safe in banks, and they rushed to take it out. As a result many banks closed, and some people never got their money.

Van Buren responded to the panic by suggesting the government create an organization to collect and manage the government's money. This organization, which he called the Independent Treasury, would keep the government's money safe. However, many bankers profited from the interest that the government's money made in the private banks, and they fought the Independent Treasury. Although it was not created until 1840, it served the country for about 70 years.

1

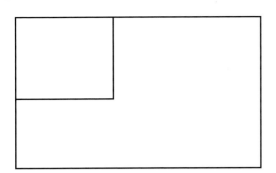

At the time Van Buren was president, there were only 26 states in the United States. To draw the 26-star flag, start with a large rectangle. Then draw a smaller rectangle in the left hand corner of the large rectangle.

2

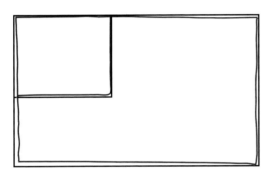

Outline the inside of the rectangles you just drew in step 1 using wavy lines as shown.

3

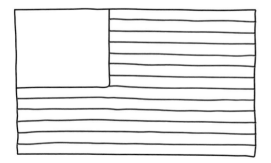

Erase the lines that are outside of the outline you created in step 2. Draw 12 wavy lines for the stripes of the flag as shown.

4

Draw the first 13 stars on the flag. These stars will be inside the smaller rectangle. There are seven stars in the top row and six stars in the second row.

5

Draw the next 13 stars. The third row of stars should have six stars in it. The last row should have seven.

6

Finish your flag by shading. Every other row of stripes should be shaded in dark. The rectangle behind the stars should also be shaded in dark. Your flag looks great!

Presidential Problems

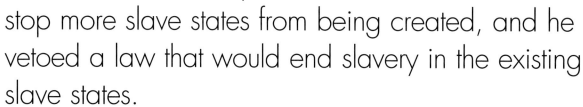

Slavery was becoming a problem for President Van Buren and his advisers. States on opposing sides argued constantly. Van Buren tried to calm both sides. He promised to stop more slave states from being created, and he vetoed a law that would end slavery in the existing slave states.

Van Buren also had problems with the Native Americans. When Andrew Jackson was president, he signed the Indian Removal Act. This act said the Native Americans who lived in the East had to move west of the Mississippi River, or they would be removed by force. Since the government wanted to build on Native American land, Van Buren maintained this law. He had peace medals, like the one shown above, made as signs of friendship and gave them to Native American leaders to convince them to move peacefully. The largest group forced to move was the Cherokee nation. Their 1838 journey west is called the Trail of Tears because of the suffering they bore.

1

Start by drawing a large circle. This will be the edge of the Van Buren peace medal.

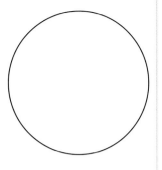

2

Draw two circles just inside the circle from step 1. Then add two smaller circles, one on top of the other, as shown. These will be the guides for the head and body of Martin Van Buren.

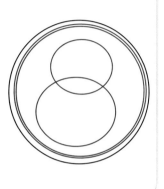

3

Add a squiggly line inside the top guide you made in step 2 for the head.

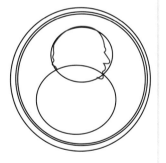

4

Add lines to Martin Van Buren's neck and body inside the bottom circle as shown. Note the slanted line used for his shirt.

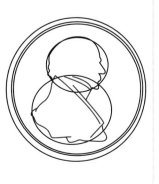

5

Erase the circle guides. Add a wavy line inside the head for the hair. Add a circle for the eye. Add two lines for the mouth and eyebrow. Start the writing along the edge of the coin.

6

Add more writing to the coin as shown. Using curved and slanted lines, add the remaining details to the face as shown. Draw curved lines on the clothing.

7

Erase the guides for the face you made in step 5. Finish the writing inside the coin. Add more lines to the clothing and the face.

8

Finish by shading. Nice work! You have completed Martin Van Buren's peace medal.

Politics After the Presidency

Many people blamed Van Buren for the problems that occurred during his presidency. He ran for reelection in 1840, but he lost to William Henry Harrison. When his term ended, Van Buren toured many of the states. He was delighted to see that many people still supported him. In 1844, he tried to win the Democratic nomination for president, but he did not succeed.

Soon a new political party called the Free Soil Party became active in New York. Their goal was to make sure that slavery would not be allowed in more states. Van Buren agreed with the goals of the Free Soil Party. In 1848, he ran for president as the Free Soil candidate. He did not expect to win, but he felt that the cause of the Free Soil Party was important. Though he lost the election, the ideas of the Free Soil Party gave people new ways to think about the issue of slavery. The above poster was used in Van Buren's 1848 presidential campaign.

1

To draw Lady Liberty from the top of Van Buren's 1848 campaign poster, start by drawing a square. This will be your guide for the drawing.

2

Add two horizontal rectangles inside the square, one on top of the other. Make sure the top rectangle is shorter. Draw a curved line on top of the two rectangles you just made.

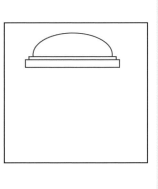

3

Add four rectangles. These will be guides for the columns. Draw straight lines to make a guide for the body. Add circular guides for the head and hands.

4

Draw columns inside the guides as shown. Draw six overlapping circles along the bottom as shown. These will be your guides for the clouds.

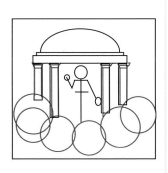

5

Erase the guides for the columns. Draw a squiggly outline around the guide for the body. Add details to the arms and hands. Add a squiggly line inside the circular guide for the head.

6

Erase the guides for Lady Liberty and the bottom of the clouds. Add slanted lines for the staff of the torch and a squiggly line for the flame. Add lines to her clothing and face.

7

Next add the writing to the rectangle above the columns. Add curved lines for the remaining clouds. Add more squiggly lines to the clothing and the flame.

8

Erase extra lines. Finish by shading. The Free Soil Party chose to put Lady Liberty on the poster to show their belief that slaves should be free. Good work!

Lindenwald and a Busy Retirement

After losing the presidential election of 1848, Martin Van Buren retired to his farm, Lindenwald, near Kinderhook, New York. He managed his farm, spent time with his  family, and played card games. During this time at Lindenwald, Van Buren wrote a book about the history of political parties in the United States.

In 1854, Van Buren went to Europe. He traveled, met with country leaders, and wrote the story of his life, or his autobiography. When he returned to the United States, Van Buren saw that the issue of slavery continued to turn Americans against one another. He wrote an essay defending Congress's right to decide if slavery would be allowed in new territories.

In his last public speech, he supported President Lincoln's call for soldiers to stop the conflict that had started in the South. This fighting later turned into the Civil War, the war Van Buren had hoped to avoid. Van Buren died on July 24, 1862, at Lindenwald.

1

Start by drawing a large rectangle. Add four more rectangles inside as shown. These rectangles will be your guides for Martin Van Buren's home, Lindenwald.

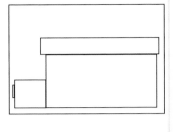

2

Add a triangle in the middle of the roof. Outline two of its sides. Add rectangles for the tower. On the leftmost shapes, add rectangles. Add two squares and triangles.

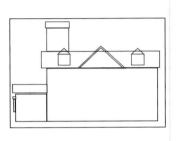

3

Draw slanted lines inside some of the guides for the roof shapes and the right side of the house. Add a rectangle as a door guide. Draw horizontal lines across the building.

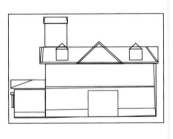

4

Draw rectangles for the door. Add a trapezoid above this. Erase extra lines. Add lines to the roofs, tower, and windows. Add a chimney. Add lines to the house as shown.

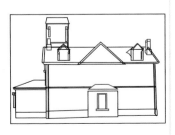

5

Erase extra lines in the windows, the chimney, and the triangle. Using rectangles and curved shapes, add windows. Add rectangles for the railings as shown.

6

Add lines for the stairs and detail to the roof. Add details to the windows and doorway as shown. Study the drawing carefully and work slowly as you add each shape.

7

Erase the trapezoid's base. Add detail to the shape over the door. Add straight lines to all of the windows. Add lines for the railing. Draw the shape to the right of the steps.

8

Add the remaining details to the roofs and doorway as shown. Then erase the rectangle guide you made in step 1. Finish by shading. Nice work!

The Little Magician

Martin Van Buren was an inspiring political leader. He was one of the first politicians to understand how dangerous the issue of slavery would become. He worked hard to find an agreement so that America could avoid going to war over the issue.

Van Buren also changed the idea of political parties. Before Van Buren, political parties were disorganized. They were simply groups of people who had similar ideas. Van Buren realized that if those people organized themselves, they could get more done. He saw that the idea of a majority rule was needed. This meant that once the majority of members agreed on an issue, the entire party needed to support it. This helped make political parties strong and unified.

Van Buren knew that to do great things people needed to cooperate with one another. His ability to get people to work together closely for their goals earned him the nickname "The Little Magician."

1

To draw Martin Van Buren's picture, start by drawing three rectangles as shown. These will be the edges of the frame.

2

Add two ovals for the inside of the frame. Then add two circles inside the ovals you just made. These will be the guides for the head and body of Martin Van Buren.

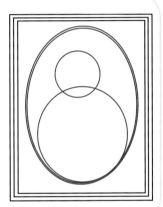

3

Add an outline for the head and the body inside the circle guides you made in step 2.

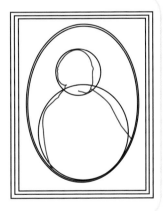

4

Erase the circle guides. Add ovals inside the shape for the arm. Add a rounded shape for the hand. Draw guides for the eyes, nose, and mouth. Draw two squiggly lines for the hair.

5

Use the guides to draw the eyes, nose, and mouth. Draw squiggly lines inside the ovals for the sleeve and hand. Add lines for the jacket collar. Add a rough vertical line for the other sleeve.

6

Erase the guides for the arm, hands, and face. Add more lines to the face. Add more lines to the clothing.

7

Add the remaining lines to the face and clothing as shown. Draw squiggly lines in each corner of the rectangle you made in step 1. These will be the decorations in the frame.

8

Finish the portrait by shading as shown. This photograph of Van Buren was created by Mathew Brady in 1856. Wonderful work!

Timeline

1782   Martin Van Buren is born on December 5 in Kinderhook, NY.

1796   At the age of 14, Van Buren begins working as a clerk in a law office.

1803   Van Buren passes his exams and becomes a lawyer at the age of 20.

1807   Van Buren marries his cousin Hannah Hoes.

1808   After helping DeWitt Clinton get reelected as mayor of New York City, Van Buren is rewarded with a job as a government clerk.

1812   After winning the election for New York state senate, Van Buren moves to Albany.

1816–1819   Van Buren serves as attorney general of New York.

1817–1825   New York State builds the Erie Canal.

1821   Van Buren is elected to the U.S. Senate and moves to Washington, D.C.

1824   Van Buren replaces Clinton as canal commissioner of the Erie Canal.

1828   Van Buren is elected governor of New York. Later this year he resigns to become President Jackson's secretary of state.

1836   Van Buren is elected president.

1837   The downfall in the country's economy, called the Panic of 1837, begins right after Van Buren takes office.

1839   Van Buren buys farmland in Kinderhook, NY. This farmland is where he will build Lindenwald. Lindenwald is now a national historic area.

1840   Van Buren runs for reelection and loses to William Henry Harrison.

1848   Van Buren runs for president as the Free Soil candidate. He loses the election.

1862   Van Buren dies at Lindenwald on July 24 during the American Civil War.

Glossary

cabinet (KAB-nit) A group of people who act as advisers to important government officials.

campaign (kam-PAYN) A plan to get a certain result, such as to win an election.

dangerous (DAYN-jer-us) Able to cause harm.

debts (DETS) Things that are owed.

economy (ih-KAH-nuh-mee) The way in which a country or a business manages its supplies and energy sources.

inaugurated (ih-NAW-gyuh-rayt-ed) To have been sworn into office.

influence (IN-floo-ens) Ability to sway others without using force.

informed (in-FORMD) To have given knowledge about something to someone else.

inspiring (in-SPYR-ing) Able to fill you with excitement.

interest (IN-ter-est) The extra cost that someone pays in order to borrow money.

involved (in-VOLVD) Kept busy by something.

lawyer (LOY-er) A person who gives advice about the law and speaks for people in court.

loyal (LOY-ul) Faithful to a person or an idea.

nomination (nah-mih-NAY-shun) A suggestion that someone should be given an award or a position.

nullify (NUH-luh-fy) To make valueless.

political parties (puh-LIH-tih-kul PAR-teez) Groups of people who have similar beliefs in how the government affairs should be run.

profited (PRAH-fit-ed) Gained or benefited in some way.

resigned (rih-ZYND) To have stepped down from a position.

responded (rih-SPOND-ed) To have answered something.

retirement (ree-TYR-ment) The giving up of an office or other career.

unified (YOO-nih-fyd) Joined together.

valuable (VAL-yoo-bul) Important, or worth lots of money.

vetoed (VEE-tohd) Turned down laws suggested by a branch or department of government.

Index

Web Sites

Due to the changing nature of Internet links, PowerKids Press has developed an online list of Web sites related to the subject of this book. This site is updated regularly. Please use this link to access the list:
www.powerkidslinks.com/kgdpusa/vanburen/